Singing Birds and Flashing Fireflies

by Dorothy Hinshaw Patent
illustrations by Mary Morgan

Franklin Watts

New York   London   Toronto   Sydney

1989

For Janet Chenery
—D.H.P.

For my son Dylan
—M.M.

Library of Congress Cataloging-in-Publication Data

Patent, Dorothy Hinshaw.
Singing birds and flashing fireflies.

(Discovering science)
Summary: Illustrates how animals use a variety of
signals to communicate with each other.
1. Animal communication—Juvenile literature.
[1. Animal communication]   I. Morgan, Mary,
1957-   ill. II. Title III. Series: Discovering
science (Franklin Watts, Inc.)
QL776.P37 1989   591.59   89-9081
ISBN 0-531-10717-5

People talk to each other every day. When you tell a friend to meet you at the playground after school, your friend understands and joins you there. Animals, too, need ways to tell each other things, or *communicate* (Kah-mew-nih-kate).

There are different ways of communicating. People don't just use their voices. They also show how they feel with a smile, a frown, a friendly pat on the back, or a kiss. Like people, animals need to "talk" to one another. But animals don't have words. So how do they communicate?

SPECIAL WAYS OF COMMUNICATING

Dogs bark or growl. Horses neigh. Male crickets rub their wings together to make the chirping sounds that attract females. Some fish grate their teeth together to make sounds.

Many animals use their tails to show how they feel. Some crabs and spiders wave their legs in special patterns to attract a mate.

Dogs, horses, and cats use their ears not only to hear but also to show how they are feeling. They flatten them back if they are angry or let them stand straight up if they are alert, eager, or happy.

SINGING BIRDS

Have you ever heard the lovely song of a sparrow in the morning? When birds sing, they are not just making beautiful music. They are communicating.

While female birds can chirp, it is usually the males that truly "sing." Sometimes they sing to attract a mate—"This is my place. Here I am, ready to start a family."

Once a songbird and his mate get together, the male sings for a different reason. Now he is letting other birds of his kind know where his home is. His song says, "This is my place. Stay away."

Each kind of songbird has its own special song. When you hear certain notes, you know that you are listening to a white-crowned sparrow. A meadowlark has a very different tune. Each bird can recognize when another bird of its own kind is singing.

When birds sing, they are not using real language the way humans do. While humans can speak hundreds of different languages, each kind of bird has only one "language" with a few "words."

We can tell each other all kinds of things
with words. But birds have only a few messages
they can get across. A person can say the same
thing in different ways. "Please come to my
birthday party on Saturday" means the same as
"Saturday is my birthday. Can you come to my
party?" But a bird has only one way of saying
"This is my place."

FLASHING FIREFLIES

Many animals depend more on sight than sound to get messages across. The sparkling flashes of fireflies across a nighttime meadow are beautiful to us. But they provide important information to the fireflies.

During the mating season, female fireflies often perch on the tops of plants, while the males fly above them, flashing bright signals.

There are many kinds of fireflies, and each kind has its own special flashing code. When a female sees the proper code, she waits just the right amount of time. Then she flashes back.

When a male sees a flash from the grass at the right time, he turns and heads to the spot. Here is a female of his kind, ready to mate with him. As he approaches, he flashes again and she answers. When he gets close, he lands on the grass and walks toward her, flashing as he comes. Then they mate.

DANGER!

One important message to communicate is danger. Mother animals have good ways of warning their young. A mother fox warns of danger with a bark. Some birds use high, thin whistles to alert their babies that danger is near.

Animals that live in herds or colonies also have ways of communicating alarm. A frightened white-tailed deer raises its tail, revealing a startling white patch on the rear that can be seen for quite a distance.

Prairie dogs and ground squirrels that live in colonies give out alarm whistles. One kind of whistle means that an enemy is approaching on the ground. A different call warns of danger from some bird flying overhead.

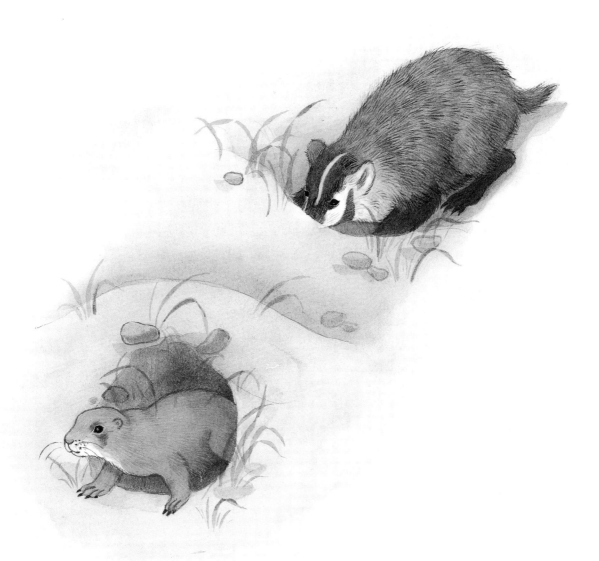

Some squirrels even have one signal for a digging enemy, such as a badger, and a different signal for an animal that can't dig very well, such as a coyote. To escape from a badger, a squirrel needs to run to a burrow with two openings so it can escape if the badger tries to dig it out. Any burrow will do to escape a coyote, since the coyote can't dig very well.

TRAILING ANTS

Have you ever watched a trail of ants marching across the kitchen floor toward a bit of food, or heading out from a woodland nest? The ants are traveling in both directions, hurrying along their way. Some of them are going out from the nest. Others are returning with something to eat.

How do the ants know where to go to find the food?

Many ants live in big nests underground, or above the ground in wood. There are thousands of them in each of these big family homes. Some of the ants wander away from the nest looking for food. They are called scouts.

When a scout finds a juicy piece of fruit, a dead grasshopper, or some other food, it heads for home. As it returns, the scout leaves a trail with a special chemical released from the rear end of its body.

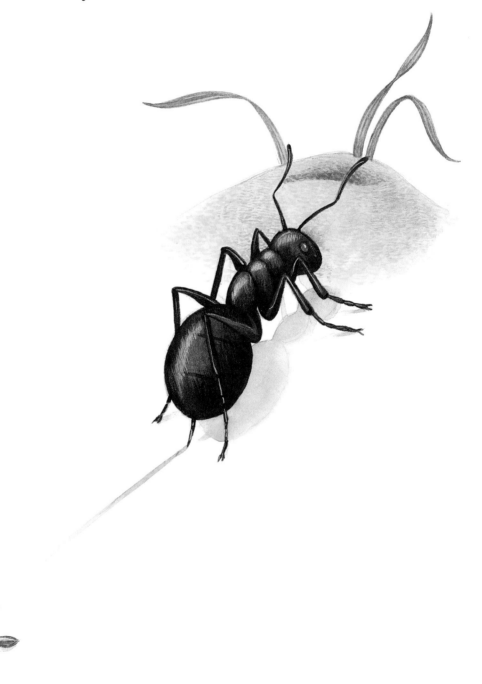

Back at the nest, other ants smell the fresh trail left by the scout. They follow it back to the food.

After collecting as much as they can carry,
they scurry back to the nest, leaving more of the
chemical trail as they go.

Every ant that returns with food leaves a
trail, just like the scout. More and more ants
head out and return with good things to eat.

Once all the food is gone, returning ants no longer leave any scent on their way home. The trail smell gets weaker and weaker, and soon the ants don't waste any more time following it.

A LOVING TOUCH

Wolves live in very close groups called packs. They have many different ways of communicating with each other.

They do so by howling, moving their ears
and tails, and using smell. But for wolves, touch
is also a very important way of expressing
feelings.

In each wolf pack, one male and one female
are the leaders. The other wolves are usually
their offspring from different years.

When one of the leaders has been away for a while and returns, the other wolves dash over to greet the returning wolf.

They nuzzle the leader. They lick at his or
her face and push their bodies as close together
as they can. Their greetings seem much like
humans' hugs and kisses.

WAYS OF "TALKING"

You can see that animals communicate in many ways. They use sight, sound, smell, and touch. Next time you go for a walk in the park or to the zoo, see if you can figure out how the animals you see are "talking" to each other.

Animals in this Book